T0402805

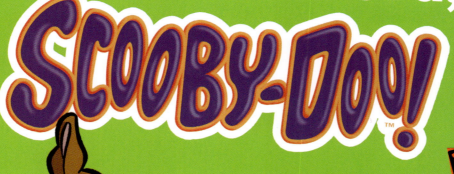

Stay Connected, SCOOBY-DOO!

A Guide to ONLINE SAFETY

by Steve Korté

PEBBLE
a capstone imprint

Published by Pebble, an imprint of Capstone
1710 Roe Crest Drive, North Mankato, Minnesota 56003
capstonepub.com

Library of Congress Cataloging-in-Publication Data
is available on the Library of Congress website.
ISBN: 9798875220593 (hardcover)
ISBN: 9798875220548 (paperback)
ISBN: 9798875220555 (ebook PDF)

Summary: From a website asking for personal information to a pop-up
ad offering free stuff, being online can be overwhelming. But Scooby-Doo
and the Mystery Inc. gang are ready to calm your fears with lots of safety tips.

Image Credits
Getty Images: Cavan Images/Natalie Brenner, 8, Deagreez, 25, fad1986, 7 (laptop),
fleaz (doodles), 1 (top) and throughout, Herwin Bahar, 17, JackF, 10, LauriPatterson, 27,
Mahmud013, cover, Maskot, 18, monkeybusinessimages, 22, PictureNet Corporation, 20,
RedVector, 26 (screen and icons), Ridofranz, 24, Tran Van Quyet, 28; Shutterstock: alexmillos,
16 (screen inset), Dragon Images, 4, JaturunThakard, 16, Kanoktuch, 15, lookmanhakim,
13, Monkey Business Images, 12, New Africa, 14, Nikola Stanisic, 26, Polina Tomtosova
(doodles), 11 and throughout, Rawpixel, 7 (screen inset), renko_art (doodles), 1 (bottom) and
throughout, Roman Samborskyi, 5, 21, TimeImage Production, 6, watercolor 15 (notepad),
back cover and throughout, Yurii_Yarema, 9

Editorial Credits
Editor: Christianne Jones; Designer: Bobbie Nuytten; Media Researcher:
Svetlana Zhurkin; Production Specialist: Katy LaVigne

Printed and bound in China. 6274

The Mystery Inc. team has been keeping people all over the world safe from monsters and ghosts. But it's not easy to keep people safe online.

Online safety means keeping yourself and others safe when you visit websites, play digital games, or connect with other people on the internet. When you don't know what to do, just ask Scooby-Doo!

Hey, look! Someone left the computer on. I would love to check out some cool websites or download a new app.

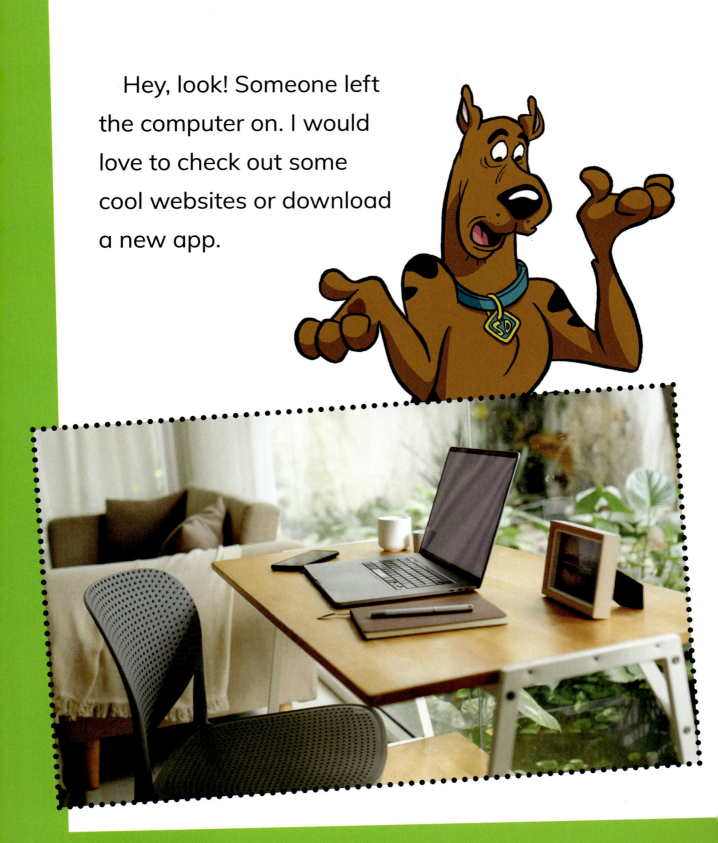

You should always ask a grown-up before going online. It's not because you aren't trusted. It's because not all websites and apps can be trusted.

My friend told me to check out a new online game, but it's asking for my personal information. I *really* want to play the game.

Always ask a trusted caregiver before sharing anything online. And never share your name, address, or school on a website. It's like a stranger knocking on your door. You never know who is on the other side.

FRED'S WEBSITE SAFETY REMINDERS

- Never open a new website without an adult's okay.

- Never share personal information without an adult's approval.

- Never share photos of yourself or others without getting permission.

A pop-up ad just appeared on a site I'm viewing. It's offering a free online version of my favorite video game. All I have to do is click the link for more details.

You should never click on a link or download anything without getting an adult's permission. Clicking on a link could download a virus that could break your computer or phone.

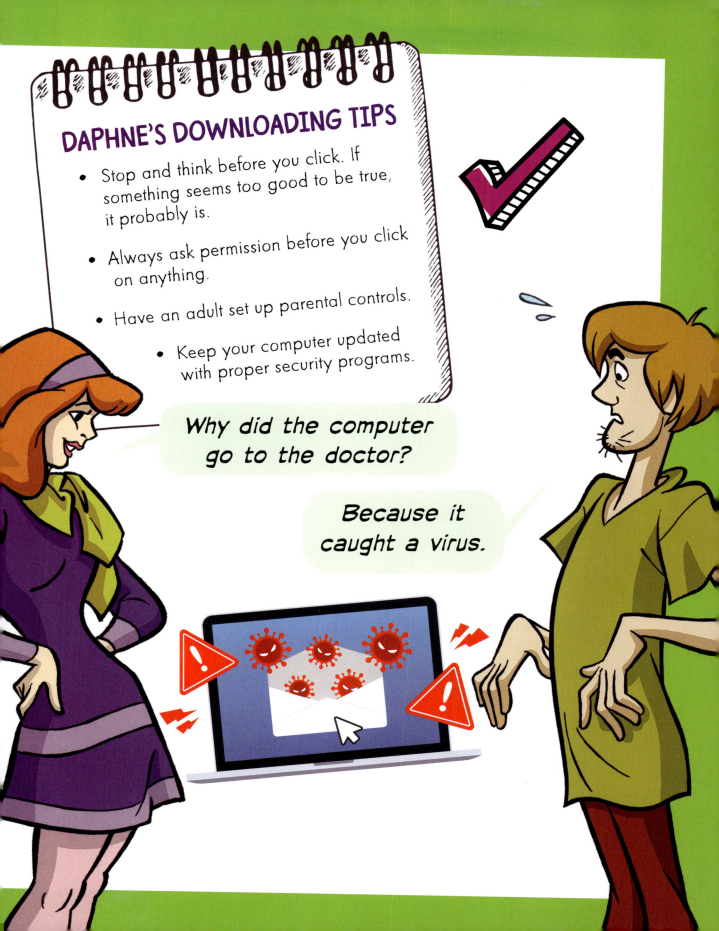

I got permission from an adult to visit a new website. It's telling me that I need to set up a password.

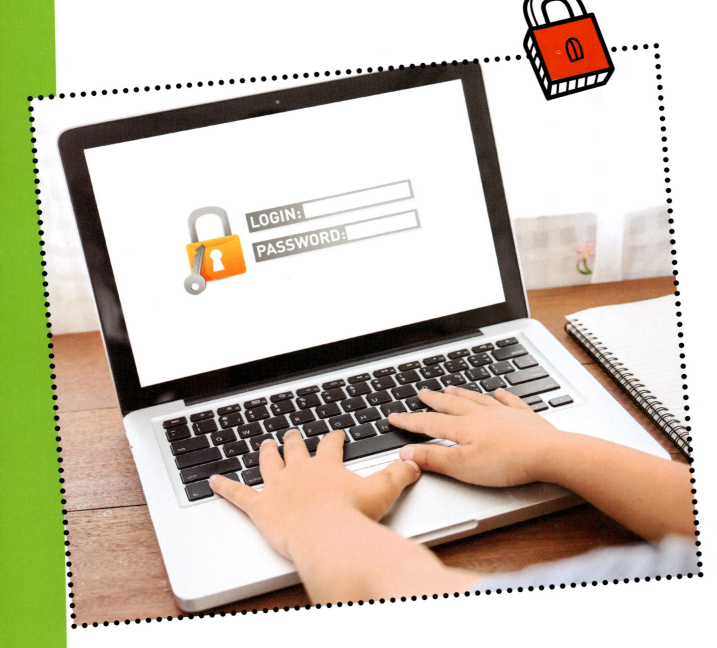

Ask an adult to help you set up a password. Computer passwords are like secret codes that keep your information safe. They protect your games, pictures, and messages.

DON'T FORGET!

A password is meant to keep you and your information safe. Don't share it with anyone except grown-ups you trust.

VELMA'S PASSWORD TIPS

- Use a mix of numbers, symbols, and uppercase and lowercase letters.

- Change your password when prompted.

- Don't use easy-to-guess options like your name or names of family members or pets, your birthday, the word "password," or any other personal information.

I just got an email from someone
I don't know. The person seems nice,
and I like to make new friends.

SCOOBY-DOO,
what should I do?

Always ask an adult before chatting with someone new online. They could ask for your personal information or try to trick you into doing something you shouldn't.

I started following my favorite singer online. I left a comment on her latest song telling her how much I like it. Then a kid at school left a comment saying that song was awful, and I was weird to like it.

People say things online that they would never say in person. A person who likes to start fights and annoy people online is called a "troll." The best thing you can do is not feed an online troll by responding to their comments.

Scooby-Doo and the gang want you to have fun and safe online experiences. Be sure to take their advice and follow these SAFE rules.

Stay away from strangers online.

Ask an adult before going online.

Follow family rules for using a computer or phone.

Exit any websites or chats that ask for your personal information.

Scooby-Doo's
Online Safety Review

1. Who should you ask before you go online?

a. your dog

b. your best friend

c. a trusted adult

2. What is a person who likes to start fights online called?

a. a troll

b. a monster

c. a rat

3. Why should you use a password?

a. because it's fun

b. to keep your data safe

c. to hide things from your parents

4. What is one thing you should use in your password?

a. symbols

b. your name

c. your address

5. When is it okay to message a stranger?
   a. once a week
   b. whenever you want
   c. never

6. What should you do if you see a pop-up ad?
   a. show an adult
   b. click it
   c. shut off your computer immediately

7. When should you change your password?
   a. every day
   b. when prompted
   c. never

8. What is the best overall rule for online safety?
   a. have fun all the time
   b. don't worry about passwords
   c. always ask an adult

ANSWERS: 1. c 2. a 3. b 4. a 5. c 6. a 7. b 8. c

How many signs can YOU find?

There are different warning signs throughout this book. See how many of each you can find!

About the Author

Steve Korté is the author of more than 100 books, featuring characters like Batman, Bigfoot, and the Loch Ness Monster. As a former editor at DC Comics, he worked on hundreds of titles, including *75 Years of DC Comics*, *Wonder Woman: The Complete History*, and *Jack Cole and Plastic Man*. He lives in New York City with his husband Bill.